ONCE UPON A TEXAS

Seven short plays about life in Stephen F. Austin's Colony

plus

PECOS BILL AND THE TEXAS STARS

a humorous play from folklore

by

I. E. CLARK

I. E. Clark, Inc.
Schulenburg, TX 78956

Printed in the United States of America

ISBN 0-88680-238-5

ONCE UPON A TEXAS

Cast

Texas Between the Rivers

Voice (man or woman)
Deer (woman, preferably)
Indian Brave
Indian Squaw
Frenchman (man or woman)
Spaniard (man or woman)
Stephen F. Austin
W. B. Dewees
Jim

Texas by Any Other Name

(Performers may be all women)

Announcer
Tejas, *a pretty Indian maiden (small)*
*Karankawa, *a hungry Indian maiden (large)*
†Tonkawa, *an Indian maiden (middle-sized)*
Other Indians (men or women)
§Frenchman (man or woman)
†Spanish Senorita
*Spanish Explorer (man or woman)
‡Mexican Peasant (man or woman)
§Fishing Pole Girl
*Indian Girl
†Spanish Maiden
‡Pioneer Maiden
*, †, §, ‡ may be double cast

A Capital Idea

(Performers may be all men)

Announcer (man or woman)
Stephen F. Austin
Baron de Bastrop
Helper 1 (man or woman)
Helper 2 (man or woman)
W. B. Dewees
Benjamin Beason
Messenger (man or woman)

It Takes a Heap of Lovin'

Announcer (man or woman)
2 to 6 Pioneer Men
2 to 6 Pioneer Women

Life in the Country

Announcer (man or woman)
9 Pioneer Men
7 to 8 Pioneer Women
3 Children (boys or girls)

Those Revolting Texians

Announcer (man or woman)
3 Soldiers
3 Runaways (men)
1 Lost Woman
Sam Houston
Captain Juan Seguin
W. B. Dewees

Three-Legged Willie

Announcer (man or woman)
* 2 Men
2 Women
Judge Williamson
Deputy
Sheriff Stephen Townsend
Abner Bibbs, *a cattle rustler*
* 6 Jurymen
Citizens (all men, all women or some of each)
* the two men may be part of the jury

Pecos Bill and the Texas Stars

Announcer (man or woman)
* 1 or 2 Mules (men or women)
Pecos Bill
Coyote (man or woman)
* Sue
* Widowmaker (strong man or woman)
Other coyotes if desired (men and/or women)
Singers (men and/or women)
* may double

ABOUT THE PLAY

The story of Texas Independence is as important to world history as the revolt of the Thirteen American Colonies. At opposite ends of what is now the United States, the two revolutions occurred within 70 years of each other. The two sets of rebels were somewhat similar–George Washington and Sam Houston, for example, and Stephen F. Austin and Benjamin Franklin. Many Mexicans fought on the side of Texas in 1836 just as many Englishmen fought for America in 1776.

The cause of the two revolutions was the same–a fight by common people for freedom from tyranny. The rebel armies were similar–untrained farmers battling well-trained, well-organized warriors. And the erstwhile enemies–England and Mexico–are now friends of the U. S. A. and Texas.

But there are differences, too. More than 150 years went by from the landing of John Smith at Jamestown in 1607 and the Pilgrims at Plymouth Rock in 1620 to the signing of the American Declaration of Independence in Philadelphia in 1776. But only 15 years passed from the establishment of Austin's first colony in 1821 to the signing of the Texas Declaration of Independence at Washington-on-the-Brazos in 1836. It took the American Colonists seven years after their declaration to defeat the British; it took the Texans less than two months to defeat the Mexicans. The battle at Yorktown, which ended the American Revolution, lasted 13 days. The Battle of San Jacinto, which ended the Texas Revolution, lasted 18 minutes.

George Washington's army had a strong ally in France. The Texans had no allies. Americans in the U. S. were rooting for their sons and brothers in Texas–but they sent little if any help. There are similarities in the "Shot heard round the world" which opened the American Revolution at Lexington, Mass., on April 19, 1775, and the "Come and Take It" battle at Gonzales, which opened the Texas Revolution on October 2, 1835 . . . but the American Revolution had nothing to compare to the Battle of the Alamo or the massacre at Goliad.

It is intriguing to speculate what might have happened if the American Colonists had not separated from England. Would Texas have become a British colony, too? Or would there now be a United States of Texas?

The seven playlets in this book give a fictional but more or less true picture of what life was like in Stephen F. Austin's original colony from its earliest settlers to the establishment of the Republic of Texas. The eighth short play in this collection—"Pecos Bill and the Texas Stars"—depicts the fanciful "invention" of the Lone Star State by its most famous folklore character, Pecos Bill, and his wild, wild bronco, Widow-maker.

The historical sketches are based on research for a Columbus, Texas, Sesquicentennial Pageant commissioned by Columbus Homes Tours, Inc. for the 150th birthday of the city of Columbus, Texas, in 1973, and a Fayette County Historical Pageant commissioned by the Fayette County Commissioners Court for presentation during the Texas Sesquicentennial in 1986. The author extends appreciation and gratitude to Mrs. Philip Gates and Mr. and Mrs. LeRoy Stein, Columbus pageant chairmen and coordinators; to Mrs. P. K. Shatto and her research committee for the Columbus Sesquicentennial; and to Mr. Walter P. Freytag of La Grange and his research committee for the Fayette County Historical Pageant; and to all others who helped bring these decisive moments in Texas and American history to life. The playlets:

1) Texas Between the Rivers is about W. B. Dewees, one of the first settlers in Austin's Colony, as he and a companion explored the Colorado River between what are now the cities of La Grange and Columbus. Dewees is called "The Father of Columbus." This sketch shows the loneliness of pioneer life and the constant danger from snakes and wild animals and Indians. It also shows the humor with which the early settlers had to flavor their courage to make life bearable.

2) Texas by Any Other Name is a colorful production number about the naming of Texas and some of its rivers, giving the Indian, French, Spanish, and English names.

3) A Capital Idea features Stephen F. Austin and the Baron de Bastrop in a humorous episode about choosing the site of Austin's capital, San Felipe de Austin.

4) It Takes a Heap of Lovin' is a specialty dance episode depicting several men building a log cabin while the women provide refreshments.

5) Life in the Country is a poignantly dramatic portrayal of the hardships and dangers of pioneer life in Texas. The daily struggle to find food and protect the settlements from Indians was made even harder by the drouth of 1824, the year in which this episode is laid. While an announcer tells the story, performers act it out in mime.

6) Those Revolting Texians portrays the first shot of the Texas Revolution with the "Come and Take It" cannon at Gonzales, the

Runaway Scrape following the fall of the Alamo, and Sam Houston planning his strategy during his "retreat to victory" toward San Jacinto. Drama, tragedy, and humor blend to make this significant episode in Texas history live for your audiences.

7) Three-Legged Willie gives a humorous look at the first district court in the Republic of Texas–under a liveoak tree in Columbus–Judge Williamson presiding.

You may present one, all eight, or any combination of the playlets. Each playlet runs 5 to 15 minutes; the seven historical sketches fit together well for a full evening's entertainment, as well as a tribute to the men and women who gave us Texas as we know it today. "Pecos Bill and the Texas Stars" provides a lively, cheerful conclusion to the seven historical sketches.

The same performers may be used in all the playlets, or a different cast may be chosen for each, which means that a fairly small or a very large group of actors may appear on stage.

The plays are suitable for all groups and all ages.

ONCE UPON A TEXAS

1. Texas Between the Rivers

[The curtain opens on darkness; from the depths we hear primeval music (perhaps "Uirapuru" by Villa-Lobos, or other jungle-like music from Villa-Lobos–or perhaps just the rhythm of drums). Then a voice booms through the darkness, like the voice of God (see Production Notes at the back of this book for suggestions for special effects, costumes, scenery, etc.)]

VOICE. Hidden in the distant folds and crevices of time, there was a beginning . . . *[LIGHTS begin to gradually dim up until we can see the outlines of trees (profile pieces)]* The land was young and the trees were small. And then the animals came. *[LIGHTS get brighter. Perhaps we hear bird songs. A DEER peeps out from behind a tree–a cute, wide-eyed dear little deer. It sees nothing and steps out cautiously from behind the tree, crosses Down Center, sees the audience, stares in horror, turns and dashes off Stage Left]* A few thousand centuries went by, and people came . . . *[The DEER runs in from Stage Left and speeds across the stage, followed by an INDIAN BRAVE aiming a bow and arrow, accompanied by Indian music or chants]* . . . Indians . . . *[The DEER and BRAVE run off Right. An INDIAN SQUAW runs in at Left waving a rolling pin in the air. She disappears Right and immediately returns dragging the INDIAN BRAVE by the ear. They stop at Center. SQUAW waves her rolling pin threateningly]*

SQUAW. I'll teach you to chase women.

BRAVE. Ugh! I wasn't chasing women.

SQUAW. Oh, no? My neighbor said she saw you running after a little dear.

BRAVE. That's right–I was chasing a little deer–D-E-E-R.

SQUAW. What's this "D-E-E-R"? You know Indians haven't learned to read or write or spell yet.

BRAVE. A deer–a four-legged animal–for your supper.

SQUAW. Oh, dear! *[Hugs him so tight it hurts him]* Oh, my dear! *[DEER peeps out from behind tree and laughs, with her hand over her mouth. BRAVE and SQUAW exit Left, arm in arm. The DEER tiptoes after them]*

VOICE. And then the French explorers came . . . *[FRENCHMAN enters from Stage Right, wiping the sweat from his brow and slapping at mosquitoes. He looks at the trees and says:]*

FRENCHMAN. This sure is different from Paris. *[He hears a noise behind him, and runs off Right, followed by the DEER, who enters at Left running for her life. She is being chased by the BRAVE aiming his bow and arrow, and he is followed by the SQUAW wielding her rolling pin. All exit Right]*

VOICE. And the Spanish explorers . . . *[The FRENCHMAN comes running on from Stage Right, followed by the DEER, the BRAVE, the SQUAW, and a SPANIARD. All exit Left except the SPANIARD, who stops at Down Center and unrolls a treasure map]*

SPANIARD. Donde está el oro? *[He scratches his head, looks around, and begins creeping off Left in search of gold]*

VOICE. . . . in search of gold. And then came the Americans . . . like Stephen F. Austin. *[STEPHEN F. AUSTIN appears at Stage Right, also with a map–a survey map, not a treasure map. AUSTIN looks at the map and then crosses to Center and inspects the area with his eyes, nodding approval]* Texas today is a land between the rivers–the Red on the north, the Sabine on the east, and the Rio Grande on the south and west. But the American colonization of Texas started out between two other rivers, the Colorado and the Brazos, where Mexican law allowed Austin to grant land to families.

AUSTIN. It looks like this acreage ought to support about 300 families. I'll wager that someday they'll be called "The Old Three Hundred." *[AUSTIN walks off Left]*

VOICE. A few bachelors managed to get grants, however, and they were among the first Yankees to explore along the two rivers. Say, here come two of them now: *[W. B. DEWEES enters Right; JIM enters Left. They see each other, approach, and hold out hands to shake]* This is probably the first time in Texas history that one Texan greeted another with . . .

DEWEES. Howdy, pardner.

JIM. Where the cuss word have you been, Dewees! I've been lookin' all over tarnation fer ya. It's fixin' to git dark. *[Note: JIM may use profanities instead of "cuss word"–according to your community standards and the maturity of your audiences]*

DEWEES. Been restin', Jim. That's a long trek from Kentucky.

JIM. Yeah–an' dangerous, too.

DEWEES. Well, we better git gittin'. We gotta find Beason's Ferry.

[The two men trudge in and out among the trees for a moment or two, and then return to Down Center. As they walk, stage LIGHTS dim somewhat]

JIM. Cuss word, but it's dark. Don't they have no durn moon in this part of the world? *[He staggers blindly Down Left Center–a man groping his way through pitch blackness]*

DEWEES. *[Groping his way to Down Right Center]* Man, you don't know a favor when one hits you over the head. If we cain't see nothin', then that means nothin' cain't see us.

JIM. *[When he hears Dewees's voice, he realizes he is moving away from his partner. He runs toward Dewees]* How do you mean, W. B.?

DEWEES. What's been scarin' the livin' sweat out of you ever since we left Nacogdoches?

JIM. *[Taking a step closer]* You mean– *[gulp]* –water moccasins?

DEWEES. Worse than that.

JIM. *[Another step; hoarsely]* Ra-rattlesnakes?

DEWEES. Worse than any kind of snakes.

JIM. Bears?

DEWEES. *[Crosses Down Right]* Oh, come on, Jim! *[Turns to him]* Why do you turn whiter than a cottonmouth's tonsils ever' time a twig snaps or an owl hoots?

JIM. *[Runs to Dewees]* You mean–you don't mean–cuss word, you mean there's– *[gulp, gulp; grabs hold of Dewees in fear]* –Indians!

DEWEES. I hear they're worse on the Colorado than anywheres else in Texas.

JIM. *[Groaning]* Oh-h-h!

DEWEES. *[Crosses Down Center, pointing downstream (the edge of the stage is the bank of the river)]* And the further you go downstream, the meaner they git. And the meanest ones of all is the Karankawas. They're so mean– *[turns to Jim, intentionally trying to scare him]* –they are cannibals!

JIM. *[Frozen; he can hardly speak, much less move]* You mean they– *[he can't say the words; he pantomimes eating]* . . .?

DEWEES. Yep.

JIM. People?

DEWEES. Yep. With tabasco sauce and horseradish.

JIM. *[Very carefully stepping to Dewees, looking all around him as he does so]* Are we–are we in Karankyway territory?

DEWEES. I reckon we're gittin' mighty close.

JIM. Oh-h-h-h–cuss word! *[A DOG howls faintly in the distance. There is a long moment of silence. DEWEES turns toward the sound, questioningly; JIM whispers]* Was–was that you, W. B.?

DEWEES. No–I thought it was you, still moaning. *[Silence. The HOWL comes again, louder]*

JIM. Is–is that the way a–a Karankyway sounds?

DEWEES. It sounds more like the way a dog sounds. *[Silence]* Maybe it's another settler somewhere along the river.

JIM. *[Trying–but not very successfully–to convince himself]* Yeh–bound to be. If them Karankyways is so hungry they eat *people,* they sure wouldn't have no *dogs* left. *[Nervous laugh]* Would they?

DEWEES. *[Peering off Right]* The *Tonkawas* love dogs.

JIM. *Tonkyways?!* What do *they* eat?

DEWEES. *[Facing Jim in irritation]* They only eat little kids and pretty women, Jim. Now shut up and listen! *[They listen intently. After a moment of deep silence the DOG's howl comes again]* Let's go see can we find him.

JIM. Find who?

DEWEES. That dog.

JIM. Cuss word–are you plumb crazy, W. B.?

DEWEES. Maybe. But I gotta find out who we're close to. If it's an Indian village, we better move on. If it's another settler–why, it'll be good to see somebody's face beside yours for a change.

JIM. Well, cuss word, I ain't goin' nowhere till it gits light.

DEWEES. *[Preparing to leave off Right; shoulders his rifle]* Okay. See you later. Maybe.

JIM. Wait a minute. I've decided to go. *[The two men creep off Right. As the Voice speaks, MOONLIGHT very slowly illuminates the stage. (For an interesting effect, let several colors of light filter through the trees)]*

VOICE. The published letters of W. B. Dewees tell us about the early settlers in the Colony. Dewees had just arrived at the Colorado River, and he wrote about it in these words:

DEWEES'S VOICE. *[From offstage, either recorded or spoken through a microphone]* "While we were making preparations for roasting a piece of venison, we were surprised by the barking of a dog apparently half a mile above us on the opposite side of the river. Not knowing whether it was the dog of an Indian or a white man, we shouldered our rifles and went up opposite the place from whence the sound proceeded."

[DEWEES enters Down Right, crosses Down Left Center, peering cautiously out over the heads of the audience. JIM follows close behind, obviously terrified]

JIM. *[Whispering]* W. B. *[No answer]* Hey, W. B. –what's that? *[Pointing Up Left]*

DEWEES. What's what?

JIM. That light over there in the east!

DEWEES. That's the moon, Jim. I guess it got mad because you cussed it while ago, and now it's comin' to gitcha.

JIM. That's okay, as long as the moon ain't a Karankyway. *[The MOONLIGHT becomes brighter. They continue cautiously along the bank, moving to Down Left Center; JIM is right on Dewees's heels. Suddenly DEWEES puts his hand out to stop Jim; he crouches, peers out across the river (that is, over the heads of the audience)]* Looky there, Jim.

JIM. *[Frightened]* Where! What!

DEWEES. Across the river, on that bluff.

JIM. Is it Indians?

DEWEES. Cain't you see that log cabin up there?

JIM. *[Relieved]* A log cabin! *[Uneasy again]* Do Karankyways build log cabins?

DEWEES. It's bound to be a settler. *[Stands and calls across the river]* Halloo, the cabin. Anybody home?

VOICE FROM CABIN. Halloooo across the river! Who's there?

JIM. *[Shouting for joy]* Hot cuss word, it's an American!

VOICE. Whoever you are, you better watch out.

DEWEES. For what–Indians?

JIM. *[Crouching again]* Oh, cuss word!

VOICE. No–for Stephen F. Austin. His rule for his colony says: "No drunkard, no gambler, no idler–and *no profane swearer*."

JIM. Well, I'll be cuss word. There ain't never going to be many Yankees in Texas with that rule.

BLACKOUT

II. Texas by Any Other Name

(May be played by all women)

[Curtain opens on a bare stage]

ANNOUNCER. Don't you feel sorry for the prehistoric people who lived where we live today—they didn't even know they were living in Texas! A lot of other people didn't know it either, because Texas hasn't always been called Texas. Each Indian thought of the land as his and gave it his tribal name. One of our state's favorite tribes was the Tejas Indians—but they weren't really a tribe at all. Several tribes banded together and called their alliance Tejas—which means "friends." *[A pretty, diminutive Indian maiden (TEJAS) enters, Up Center, with a profile map of Texas on which is printed TEJAS. She crosses to Down Center and kneels, holding her map and smiling amiably at the audience]*

ANNOUNCER. Another tribe was the man-eating Karankawas . . . *[A larger, muscular Indian maiden (KARANKAWA) enters, sees Tejas and creeps up behind her. KARANKAWA tucks a napkin in her neck band, takes out a carving knife and sharpening stick, and begins sharpening her knife. TEJAS doesn't see her, but continues smiling]*

ANNOUNCER. And there were the Tonkawas. *[A middle-size Indian maiden (TONKAWA) enters, Left, and just as KARANKAWA is about to begin carving Tejas, TONKAWA taps Karankawa on the shoulder. As KARANKAWA turns to look, TONKAWA hits her on the chin, knocking her out. TONKAWA pulls KARANKAWA offstage, Right]*

ANNOUNCER. There were many other tribes—Apaches and Comanches, Caddos and Yeguas, Cherokees and Wacos, who lived on the land we call Texas. *[Other INDIANS—maidens and braves—enter from various directions, doing an Indian dance. They may do a dance routine around the stage, then exit]*

ANNOUNCER. The Indians really didn't worry much about such things as giving names to spots on maps. But the European invaders began drawing maps and naming places. *[FRENCHMAN enters from Left with a French flag (optional) and a profile map of Texas. He stands at Down Right and turns his map around so we can see the lettering: LOUISIANA. Throughout this entire episode—until cue—TEJAS remains kneeling at Down Center, smiling amiably at the audience]* The French claimed the land as part of Louisiana. *[A SPANISH SENORITA enters, Right, with a Spanish flag (optional) and a Texas cutout. She crosses to Down Left, stands, and turns her map around. It reads: NEW PHILIP-*

PINES] Early Spanish explorers named it "New Philippines" in honor of their King Philip. *[A SPANISH EXPLORER enters Up Right with a Texas cutout: NEW ESTREMADURA]* Another Spanish name for the area was New Estremadura. *[The two SPANIARDS vie for position]* When the Mexicans won their independence from Spain, and the Mexican flag flew over Texas, they joined their two northern provinces and called it . . . *[MEXICAN PEASANT in serape enters with Mexican flag and Texas cutout. He crosses to the fighting Spaniards, kicks them; they fall at Down Left. Then he crosses and kneels on Tejas's left side. He turns his map around; it reads: COAHUILA AND. He smiles broadly, too]*

ANNOUNCER. The state of Coahuila and Texas. *[The MEXICAN looks at the signs, realizes they read wrong. He moves to Tejas's right and kneels, still smiling]* The state of Coahuila and Texas. *[MEXICAN looks at Tejas's sign again. He stands in front of it and pantomimes writing on the sign (actually he sticks a prepared "X" over the "J"). He returns to his position; everything is now okay. He smiles at the audience]*

ANNOUNCER. "Tejas" became "Texas" because the two letters "x" and "j" are pronounced the same in Spanish–so Texas is "tay-hahss" just as Mexico in Spanish is "may-hee-ko." In those days, nobody paid much attention to spelling anyhow–just like today. *[The flag and map holders may sing and/or dance, or simply exit–running out and waving to the audience]*

ANNOUNCER. Texas rivers also have some history behind their names. A river in West Texas is one of the strangest. A Texas Ranger rode up to a dangerous-looking gorge. A friend told him it was the River of Saint Peter. The Ranger scoffed: "It looks like the Devil's River to me" –and that's what it has been called ever since. Two little rivers that enter into Matagorda Bay were discovered by LaSalle. A herd of buffalo was grazing on one of the banks and LaSalle called it "The Cow River" –"Lavaca" in Spanish.* The other river is the Navidad, which is the Spanish word for "Christmas." Did LaSalle camp there on Christmas Day? The two rivers that formed the boundaries of Austin's first colony–the Colorado and the Brazos–met a strange fate. The Colorado has had many names . . . *[GIRL enters Left carrying a cane fishing pole]*

FISHING POLE GIRL. LaSalle called it "The River of Canes." *[Giggle]* LaSalle must have been a fisherman. *[She sits on edge of apron, Down Right Center, dangling her feet off the edge and fishing in the orchestra pit]*

***Riviere aux Boeufs (River of Bullocks) in French**

PRETTY INDIAN GIRL. *[Enters, Right, flirts a bit with the audience as she crosses to Down Left Center]* The Indians called the river Pashohono. *[In a breathy voice]* Does that mean "passionate"? or *[in wide-eyed wonderment]* does it mean—"Passion—O, No!" *[She sits on apron at Down Left Center and ponders]*

SPANISH MAIDEN. *[Perhaps dressed as a nun, enters Left and crosses Down Center]* The Spanish explorers called it "El Rio de Los Brazos de Dios." *[Reverently]* "The River of the Arms of God." *[She sits on the apron Down Center, stricken with awe]*

PIONEER MAIDEN. *[Enters Right and crosses Down Center]* And the Spanish called the river to the east the "Rio Colorado"—the Red River. Some map makers mixed up the two names and labeled the Brazos "Colorado" and the Colorado "Brazos." So when you cross the Colorado, you're really crossing the Brazos. But not *really* really because what *was* the Brazos now really *is* the Colorado, and the Colorado is really... *[She grimaces in confusion and sits at Down Center to the left of the Spanish Maiden. The two look at each other, shrug their shoulders, and continue to ponder]*

ANNOUNCER. The city which is now the capital of Texas used to be known as Waterloo. So when you go to visit the governor, instead of heading for Austin on the Colorado in the heart of Texas, you *could* be going to Waterloo on the River of Canes in the state of New Estremadura. *[The GIRLS may do a song and/or dance, or merely exit, waving at the audience]*

CURTAIN

III. A Capital Idea

(May be played by all men)

ANNOUNCER. The story of Texas as we know it today really began when Stephen F. Austin was given a grant by the Mexican government to establish an Anglo-American colony between the Colorado and Brazos Rivers. What's one of the first things a man does when he finds himself in charge of a new land? He chooses a capital. Austin's first choice was a beautiful liveoak grove in a large bend of the Colorado River.

[LIGHTS come up revealing STEPHEN F. AUSTIN, the BARON DE BASTROP, and two HELPERS surveying. FIRST HELPER stretches a chain held by SECOND HELPER; BASTROP drives a stake into the ground at Center. AUSTIN is marking on a map at Up Right Center. BASTROP speaks English with a German accent interspersed with Spanish words]

BASTROP. Fifty varas from de liveoak tree to a shtake; den vest . . . *[motioning to FIRST HELPER]* . . . take your chain vest, Isaiah. *[ISAIAH is puzzled]* Vest iss de udder vay from East, dummkopf! *[The HELPERS move the chain, and continue to move it during the following dialog]*

[W. B. DEWEES and BENJAMIN BEASON, two pioneers, enter Up Left, look around. AUSTIN crosses to greet them. The three men meet at Center]

DEWEES. Howdy, Mr. Austin. What's going on? *[DEWEES and AUSTIN shake hands]*

AUSTIN. Good morning, Dewees. This is going to be the capital of my colony–San Felipe de Austin. We're surveying the townsite.

DEWEES. That's what we heard. That's why we came down the river. This here is Benjamin Beason–you remember him. He's built his cabin just up the river a piece, and he's thinkin' of puttin' in a ferry.

AUSTIN. Sounds like a good idea. With more colonists coming, it won't be long, I reckon, till we open up a road from here to the Brazos. *[Pointing East, over the heads of the audience]*

BASTROP. *[Coming to Center to join the other men. The HELPERS sit and listen]* Ja, Empresario, I t'ink de government vill approve of dot.

AUSTIN. *[To Dewees and Beason]* Oh, by the way, this is the Baron de Bastrop–the Mexican government's commissioner for this colony.

Baron, meet W. B. Dewees and Benjamin Beason—two of my first colonists to arrive. *[DEWEES and BEASON shake hands with BASTROP. The four men have worked their way to Down Center]*

DEWEES and BEASON. Howdy.

BASTROP. Wie gehts.

BEASON. How come y'all are building your capital at this here spot?

AUSTIN. Well, when my pa came to Texas in hopes of making a colony, he picked this part, along the Brazos and Colorado—and on over to the Navidad and Lavaca—as the prettiest part of the whole state of Texas and Coahuila—

DEWEES. It's the prettiest part of the whole world!

AUSTIN. *[Taking a couple of steps Left and looking out over his domain]* I thought of building at the Atascosita Crossing—about eight miles down the river—but that's already a Mexican trade route, and we just might get mixed up with government politics if we butted in down there—

BASTROP. Ja, ve don't vant to do dot.

AUSTIN. So I decided to go upstream—and when I came to this bend in the river . . . there's something about this spot. It's high enough not to be flooded, and it's got some of the best-tasting spring water in the country. *[Shrugging his shoulders and laughing a little]* Those are practical reasons, and I guess you could find them in lots of places.

BASTROP. Ja—lots of udder places.

AUSTIN. *[Gesturing off Right]* But there's some magic here. This beautiful grove of liveoak trees makes a man feel like he's found what he's spent his life dreaming about.

BEASON. Yeah, I know what you mean. I had that feeling, too. Like you wanta drive your stake in the ground and tether your future to it.

DEWEES. But ain't you worried about the Indians? They're kinda rough along the Colorado.

AUSTIN. Well, I've found most of them friendly, and I've really had no problems—

[MESSENGER staggers in from Up Right with eight arrows sticking out of his back. He is gasping—both from pain and from the exhaustion of running]

MESSENGER. Mr. Austin—Mr. Austin—the Tonkyways—they're on the rampage!

AUSTIN. Mmm. That's a shame. But I guess we have to expect that once in a while. After all, they consider this their territory. *[Examining the arrows]* We'd better get you fixed–

MESSENGER. *[Interrupting–in pain]* They burnt Christopher's cabin and kidnapped his wife and stole his horse.

DEWEES. Lord, that's awful! He's going to miss that horse.

MESSENGER. And they attacked Castleman's cabin, too!

AUSTIN. *[Suddenly more concerned than he has seemed to be up to now]* Sylvanus Castleman! Is Castleman all right?

MESSENGER. Yeah, the whole family was out in the field–

AUSTIN. You mean they left the cabin unprotected?

MESSENGER. Looks thataway.

AUSTIN. That's where I'm staying! All my horses–

MESSENGER. Yeah, that's what I came to tell y'all. They stole all your horses–and Baron Bastrop's, too–

BASTROP. *[He has been in the background, but now he rushes to the Messenger]* Ach du teufel! In San Antonio we protect our property better dan dot!

AUSTIN. *[He meditates for a while, walking away and looking at his map. DEWEES and BEASON tend Messenger's wounds. AUSTIN looks at Bastrop]* You know, Baron, I've been thinking. Most of my colonists are settling along the Brazos–

BASTROP. Si, verdad–das ist richtig. Und de peoples here are so–how you say–harassified by de Indians, I can't find nobody to help mit de surveying.

AUSTIN. *[Facing the others]* If the capital was here, the settlers on the Brazos would have to travel 30 miles to do government business.

BASTROP. Dot's sure a long vay already.

AUSTIN. That would be a mighty lot of trouble for those folks.

BASTROP. Ja, Santa Maria! Dot vould be trouble. Und around here is nutting but Indian raids–horse stealing–murder–

AUSTIN. It doesn't seem fair to my colonists–

BASTROP. Si, ja, Empresario, it don't.

AUSTIN. *[To the Helpers]* Hey, you fellows, pull up those stakes. We're going to put San Felipe de Austin on the Brazos. *[Strides out Left, followed by a happy BASTROP. DEWEES and BEASON, disappointed, remain behind. They look at each other and shrug]*

DEWEES. Oh, well, Beason–we can always build our own town here.

BEASON. Yeah, Dewees–we'll call it Beason City.

DEWEES. How about Deweesville? *[The men freeze as Announcer speaks]*

ANNOUNCER. A town *was* built there–the town we know today as Columbus. And Austin did build his capital on the Brazos and called it San Felipe de Austin. It's a state park now, near Sealy. There haven't been any Indian raids at either place for a long time.

BLACKOUT

IV. It Takes a Heap of Lovin'

ANNOUNCER. When you wanted a house in Austin's Colony in the 1820's, you didn't call up a real estate agent, or look in the want ads, or hire a contractor to build you a new one. You built it yourself. And since building a house–even a one-room log cabin–is a pretty big chore, you were glad when your neighbors showed up to help.

[CURTAIN opens. Six MEN at Stage Right are sawing, planing, and joining logs for a log cabin. (The sections of the house are pre-built and lying on two sawhorses–see Production Notes; all the "carpentry" work is in pantomime.) Six WOMEN are at Stage Left cooking. All movements –the carpentry and the cooking–are in time with the music (hoe-down music of the period, like the "Virginia Reel.")

Three MEN carry one wall to Up Center and hold it in place. The work makes them tired; they wipe the sweat from their brows. Three WOMEN bring them refreshment.

The other three MEN carry another wall to Up Center and join the two walls together (the third and fourth walls are not needed. The MEN merely pretend to work on them). They, too, are tired, and the other three WOMEN bring them refreshment. The first three MEN return to work at Stage Right and the first three WOMEN return to Stage Left.

The first three MEN bring a section of roof to Up Center–similar refreshment business, etc. The second three MEN and WOMEN return to work–every movement still in time with the music.

Second three MEN put on the remaining section of roof. Second three WOMEN bring them refreshment. First three MEN and first three WOMEN stride to Center; the other MEN and WOMEN join them there. All six couples admire the cabin, congratulate each other, etc. Then they dance a hoe-down in celebration. At the end of the dance, they sit down to rest and admire the cabin. One MAN goes up to admire the cabin at close range. He sneezes. The cabin collapses]

BLACKOUT

V. Life in the Country

ANNOUNCER. Life was rugged, and rough, and risky for the first settlers in Stephen F. Austin's colony. It took real men and devoted women to build our state. There were no 40-hour weeks or overtime pay, and holidays were almost unheard of. There was no drive-in grocery store to go to when you were hungry, and no drugstore for medicine when you were sick. Provisions were always scarce. But to make matters worse, in 1824–just a year or so after Austin's colonists began arriving–a severe drought struck Texas.

[CURTAIN opens on log cabin at Up Center with trees in the background. Eight MEN, carrying rifles, enter through the trees and gather near the door of the cabin. Another man (MAN 1) enters from the cabin with his wife (WIFE 1) and little child (CHILD 1). He kisses them goodbye and joins the other men. The nine MEN cross to Stage Center and converse in words we cannot hear. They point in various directions, finally nodding in agreement]

ANNOUNCER. Every morning a party of men went out to hunt food. No man dared go out alone, for he would certainly fall victim to the Indians.

[MAN 2, MAN 3, and MAN 4 exit Stage Left. MAN 1, MAN 8, and MAN 9 exit Stage Right; MAN 1 waves to his wife and child. They wave back and then exit into the cabin. MAN 5, MAN 6, and MAN 7 take guard positions, kneeling at Right, Left, and Down Center. WIVES 5, 6, and 7 enter (one from Up Left, one from Right, and one from Down Left) and each gives her man a bowl of soup. The MEN at Right and Left gulp theirs down. MAN 7, at Down Center, is about to eat his when a ragged little child (CHILD 2) enters, sits at his feet, and looks at him hungrily. MAN 7 turns his back on the child, but he cannot eat. He turns to the child and gives him (or her) the bowl. CHILD 2 drinks the soup ravenously. MAN 7 holds the empty bowl out to his WIFE. She shakes her head, implying, "There is no more." The WIVES exit sadly]

ANNOUNCER. Game was so scarce that the men would often hunt all day for a deer or a turkey. And too often, the hunters returned at night empty handed.

[MEN 2, 3, and 4 enter Left. Their wives (WIVES 2, 3, and 4) enter Right and cross Center to meet them. The three MEN on guard also

meet them at Center, questioningly. MEN 2, 3, and 4 hold out their empty hands, shrug their shoulders weakly, and shake their heads in sadness. The WIVES, too, are sad, but they try to cheer up their husbands. Arm in arm, each couple exits Up Right, Right, and Down Right. MEN 5, 6, 7 follow them out. WIFE 8 and CHILD 3 enter from Left and look anxiously for their husband and father. Finally, they see him coming off Right and run to greet him. MAN 8 enters Right and meets his family at Right Center. WIFE 1 and CHILD 1 have entered from the cabin and stand at Up Center, watching the reunion. CHILD 3 is hungry; he/she tugs at father's pouch. MAN 8 kneels and gives the child a tired hug. CHILD 3 opens the pouch. It is empty; the CHILD is sad and disappointed, but stoical. WIFE 8 and MAN 8 each take one of the little child's hands, and they exit Left]

ANNOUNCER. The hunters were heartsick to have to tell their wives and their little starving, half-naked children that they had found no food that day.

[WIFE 1 and CHILD 1 watch the family leave, then they look anxiously toward the Right. No one is in sight]

ANNOUNCER. But sadder still were those families whose hunters didn't return at all.

[The stage has gradually darkened. WIFE 1 realizes that her man isn't going to return. She hugs her child, and they go sadly into the cabin, alone]

BLACKOUT

VI. Those Revolting Texians

ANNOUNCER. Stephen F. Austin's colony was successful—too successful in the eyes of the Mexican government. Fearing trouble from the growing population of Americans, the government halted immigration of United States citizens to Texas in 1830. When the order was not obeyed, Austin was imprisoned in Mexico three years later, and the Texas Declaration of Independence was signed in a log cabin at Washington-on-the-Brazos on March 2, 1836. The first shot of the Texas Revolution had already been fired—in Gonzales.

[Small cannon is pushed on stage from the Left by three SOLDIERS —dressed in pioneer clothing, not military uniforms. One of the men carries a flag bearing the words "COME AND TAKE IT." The cannon is fired (see Production Notes). The SOLDIERS jump and dance with glee]

SOLDIER 1. Yay—look at 'em run!

SOLDIER 2. I guess we showed that dad-blasted Santa Anna he better not come threatenin' us Texians.

SOLDIER 3. Man, we-uns is going to be IN-DEE-PEN-*DUNT! [They drag their cannon off Right. During Announcer's next speech, several tree stumps are placed on stage]*

ANNOUNCER. But their joy didn't last for long. On March 6, 1836, General Santa Anna defeated the Texans—they called themselves Texians—at the Alamo. Sam Houston had organized an army, but the army was too small and too untrained to meet the Mexican forces. So Houston retreated eastward—and every Anglo-American east of Gonzales was running ahead of him at full speed. Nobody wanted to be left behind at the mercy of Santa Anna.

[LIGHTS flash. Three or four RUNAWAYS rush fearfully in from Up Right. They are cold, ragged, muddy, with a few pitiful belongings slung over their backs. RUNAWAY 1 crosses to a tree stump at Stage Center and sits in exhaustion]

RUNAWAY 1. They say Santa Anna's army is the biggest, meanest army ever got together in the whole world!

RUNAWAY 2. *[Slumps down beside him]* Them poor fellers in the Alamo was given no mercy. Santa Anna shot 'em down like they was tin cans on a fence rail.

RUNAWAY 1. And nobody to come and help 'em. *[RUNAWAY 3 throws down his gear beside a stump at Down Right]*

RUNAWAY 3. How far behind us do you reckon them Mexicans are? *[He sits on stump and scrapes mud off his boots]*

RUNAWAY 1. They cain't be too fur. Santa Anna ain't gonna let Houston have time to build up a army and get recruits from the U. S. *[He takes a biscuit from knapsack and munches on it]*

RUNAWAY 2. Them lousy Gonzales deserters! If they'da stayed with Houston, his army'd be big enough to do some fightin'.

RUNAWAY 1. Ain't you a deserter?

RUNAWAY 2. Shucks no! I'm just runnin' away from them Mexicans. *[Crosses to a stump at Left Center]*

RUNAWAY 3. I wish I'd never left the good old U. S. A.

RUNAWAY 2. Me, too. But thank the Lord we got across the Colorado. It ain't easy for a big army like them Mexicans to cross a river. Maybe we can rest a while. *[Sits on stump]* Lordy, I'm tired a-runnin'.

[A WOMAN'S VOICE is heard off Right pitifully calling "Robert!" The WOMAN enters, ragged, muddy, almost hysterical, still calling and frantically looking at each of the men on stage]

WOMAN. Robert! Robert! *[To Runaway 1]* Where's Robert? *[To Runaway 3]* Help me find Robert and my baby!

RUNAWAY 1. Calm down, lady. Robert who?

WOMAN. *[To Runaway 2, peering in his face, paying no attention to what the men are saying to her]* You're not Robert. Oh, somebody, help me find my husband–and my baby! *[She pays no more attention to the men, but circles the stage in a daze]* Robert! I lost them on the trail. Robert! Robert! Won't somebody please help me find my baby! *[She runs out Left hysterically]*

RUNAWAY 1. *[Rises, crossing a few steps Left]* If she can find her husband and baby–if any of the lost husbands and wives and babies ever find each other in this mob–and this mud–the good Lord still makes miracles!

[LIGHTS dim to blackout. RUNAWAYS exit in the darkness]

ANNOUNCER. The Runaway Scrape was part of the confusion into which the American colonists were thrown after the fall of the Alamo and the massacre at Goliad. Houston's army had managed to ferry a thousand refugees over the Colorado, swollen with heavy rains in that spring of 1836. They camped on the opposite bank from Beason's Ferry.

The many desertions following the tragedies at the Alamo and Goliad left Houston with barely a thousand men—a group that couldn't be called an army because they had never been trained as an army. And only a river separated them from a Mexican force of great skill and nobody knew what tremendous size. There were no other American troops anywhere else in Texas. And none were headed that way.

[LIGHTS come up on SAM HOUSTON seated on the Center tree stump, studying a map. W. B. DEWEES is ushered in by CAPTAIN JUAN SEGUIN, Right. They cross to Houston]

SEGUIN. *[Saluting]* General Houston, this is W. B. Dewees.

HOUSTON. Thanks, Captain Seguin. *[SEGUIN leaves]* Howdy, Dewees. That Juan Seguin is one of my most valuable men. I'd offer you a chair if I had one. But under the circumstances—pull up a stump and set a spell.

DEWEES. *[Looks at stump at Left Center and laughs]* I think I'll stand if you don't mind, sir.

HOUSTON. And I'll sit if you don't mind. *[Looking Dewees over]* They tell me you know this part of the river, Dewees.

DEWEES. I ought to, General—I've been livin' here since 1823. I reckon I know ever' sand bar and whirlpool.

HOUSTON. My men—the few I have—are itchin' to fight. Some because a good fight is all they live for. But most, I think, just want to get it over with . . . one way or the other.

DEWEES. If there's ever gonna be a Republic of Texas, General, you cain't afford to lose.

HOUSTON. What do you think of our chances, Dewees? Should we move on—or wait here for Santa Anna to attack us?

DEWEES. General Houston, I've lived on this bend of the river for 13 years. And I don't think there's a better place for you to meet the enemy. Tomorrow is the 26th of March, 1836. What better date for the Republic of Texas to win its right to exist—the day that Sam Houston defeated Santa Anna at the Battle of Beason's Ferry.

HOUSTON. That's a beautiful dream, Dewees. Now give me some *realistic* reasons why we ought to stay and fight here.

DEWEES. The river is fordable just a couple miles upstream—a place they call Dewees's Ford, if you don't mind my sayin' so. And just across the river is a grove of huge liveoak trees. Your army can sneak up to a hundred and fifty yards of the enemy without bein' discovered.

HOUSTON. Mmm. I see.

DEWEES. Call your men together, General. I'll lead 'em acrost the river tonight. Tomorrow can go down in history as–

HOUSTON. *[Rises, crossing slowly to his right]* Tomorrow can also go down as another day that Sam Houston tried to whip a ragged bunch of squirrel hunters into something that no sane officer would even laughingly call an army. Or tomorrow could go down as the day that a brave band of Texians forever lost their hope for independence . . .

DEWEES. When are the volunteers from Louisiana gonna arrive?

HOUSTON. They've arrived. *[Small, bitter laugh]* Both of 'em. *[Pacing]* Dewees, every man in the United States of the North wants us to win our freedom–*[turns to Dewees]* –as long as he doesn't have to risk his own neck to help us. *[Peers out across the river–that is, over the audience]* Since the Alamo and La Bahia, Santa Anna's army has grown by reputation into a man-eating monster so big and so ferocious that any man with a pea-sized brain full of common sense would be scared to fight it. *[Crosses to Left Center stump]* Nope, Dewees–*[foot on stump]* right here is the entire Republic of Texas–untrained soldiers and terrified refugees–all gathered onto this muddy bank of this–*[waves at river; pause]* –I started to say Godforsaken river . . . but I pray with all my heart that it's a God-blessed river–blessed in the favor of freedom and the right of men and women to govern themselves.

DEWEES. *[Crossing to him]* We've been building Texas for 13 years, General. We ain't gonna give up as long as there's a man of us left alive.

HOUSTON. *[Crosses to Center stump]* That's what Davy Crockett and Jim Bowie and Bill Travis said at the Alamo. *[Pause]* No, we're not going to cross the river tonight, Dewees. *[Sits on stump]* Come back and see me in the morning?

DEWEES. In your tent?

HOUSTON. *[Picks up his map]* Right here–on this tree stump. I have no tent. *[LIGHTS dim to blackout]*

ANNOUNCER. Everybody who has ever lived in Texas–and most of the rest of the world, too–knows that Sam Houston kept retreating eastward, and training his army along the way, until the Texians and the Mexicans finally met on April 21, 1836, in the Battle of San Jacinto–a battle that lasted 18 minutes. And the Lone Star flag has flown proudly over Texas ever since.

CURTAIN

VII. Three-Legged Willie

ANNOUNCER. Soon after the defeat of Santa Anna's army the settlers returned westward to their land—and to the homes that weren't there, for everything had been burned during the Texian army's long march from Gonzales to the San Jacinto River. And the goverment of the Republic of Texas began functioning. The new nation's first district court was held under a liveoak tree on the banks of the Colorado at Columbus in 1837.

[LIGHTS come up revealing a barrel and a stool beneath a liveoak tree. Numerous MEN and WOMEN are standing around waiting for court to begin]

WOMAN 1. This is a crazy place to hold court.

MAN 1. Well, there ain't no courthouse—not even a saloon—in this town. I speck this tree is as good a place as any for Three-Legged Willie to—

WOMAN 1. Who?

MAN 1. Three-Legged Willie.

WOMAN 2. Now who in tarnation is Three-Legged Willie?

MAN 1. Why, I thought everybody knew that. Three-Legged Willie Williamson—the judge!

WOMAN 2. Where'd he git a name like that?

MAN 1. You'll see.

[JUDGE WILLIAMSON enters Up Center and crosses Center. One leg is bent at the knee, and a wooden peg-leg extends from the knee to the ground, giving the effect of three legs (see Production Notes)]

WOMAN 1. Why, that's the weirdest thing I ever did see. Why does he do it?

MAN 1. Wal—I don't rightly know. He jist does.

MAN 2. A disease caused his leg to double back at the knee, so he hooked on a wooden leg. He has his pants made special.

JUDGE. *[Rapping on barrel with a stick of wood]* This district court is called to order. *[Sits on stool; the peg-leg sticks out in front of his lap]* Anybody got any complaints?

DEPUTY. *[Stepping forward]* Hey, your honor, you ain't called the veniremen.

JUDGE. How do we know we'll need a jury, Deputy? Nobody's brought up any cases yet.

DEPUTY. All the same, your honor, that's the way it's done.

JUDGE. Suits me. Deputy, call the–

MAN 1. *[Stepping up to the barrel, across from the Judge]* We don't need no court and no jury here, Judge. *[Pulls out a Bowie knife and brandishes it]* This is the law in this county. *[Stabs knife into barrel]*

JUDGE. *[Drawing his six-shooter]* And this is the constitution that over-rides the law. *[MAN 1 retreats. CROWD laughs]* Now, we going to have any more disorder in this court? *[He twirls his revolver; CROWD instantly gets quiet]* Deputy, call the venire facias.

DEPUTY. Richard Breeding *[each man steps up and answers when his name is called]*, William Burnam, Moses Townsend, James Cummings, Abram Alley, Joel W. Robinson, Robert Smith . . . *[no answer]* Robert Smith . . .?

WOMAN 2. He ain't here.

JUDGE. All absent jurors are fined $20 and ordered to appear at the next term of court to show cause why they shouldn't get worse punishment. All right, anybody got any complaints?

[SHERIFF STEPHEN TOWNSEND enters through crowd at Right, leading a PRISONER in chains]

SHERIFF. Your honor, I'm Sheriff Townsend, and this here scoundrel is a cattle thief. *[Shoves Prisoner roughly forward]*

JUDGE. What evidence do you have to offer the court, Sheriff?

SHERIFF. *[Pointing to his eyes]* These eyes, your honor. It was my cattle he stole. *[CROWD reacts at the irony]*

JUDGE. *[To the defendent]* State your name.

BIBBS. Abner Bibbs.

JUDGE. Guilty or not guilty?

BIBBS. Well, since the sheriff kotched me in the act, I reckon I better plead guilty.

JUDGE. How says the jury?

JURYMAN 1. Hang him!

OTHER JURYMEN. *[Ad lib]* Yeh, string him up! Hangin's too good for cattle rustlers. Shoot the snake! Etc.

JUDGE. Did you get your cattle back, Sheriff?

SHERIFF. Sure, your honor. Like I said, I caught him in the act of drivin' 'em off.

JUDGE. Then I guess hangin's too severe. Here's the sentence. Abner Bibbs, I sentence you to be branded with a hot iron, the letter T–

BIBBS. My name begins with a B, your honor.

JUDGE. "T" is for "thief," you ornery thief! You shall be given 39 lashes on the bare back, and you shall be fined $500 and kept in custody until the fine is paid.

SHERIFF. How we gonna keep him in custody, Judge? The jailhouse burned up with everything else.

JUDGE. Chain him to this tree.

BIBBS. *[Blanching at the idea]* But–but–where am I gonna git five hundred dollars! Judge, I'll be chained to that tree till it grows around me.

MAN 1. Your honor, I'll wager there ain't $500 in all of Texas west of the Colorado put together.

JUDGE. I guess you're right. Go git the brandin' iron and the whip, Sheriff. The fine's remitted.

BLACKOUT

ANNOUNCER. And that's the way Texas began. You know the rest of the story–annexed to the United States in 1845. Seceded and joined the Confederacy. Brought back into the Union after the Civil War. Bragged about being the biggest state in the nation until 1959 when some overgrown iceberg named Alaska joined the Union. But still brags about being the *best* state, because that's the way Texans have made it–from Stephen F. Austin and Davy Crockett and Sam Houston right up to you folks out there in the audience today. Let's keep it that way.

CURTAIN

PECOS BILL and the TEXAS STARS

PECOS BILL AND THE TEXAS STARS

[Several large cactus plants are spaced around the stage; otherwise the stage is bare]

ANNOUNCER. Once upon a time, when the Southwestern part of the U. S. A. was just a flat, bare prairie, a pioneer family traveled across the land in their covered wagon.

[Covered wagon (a small wagon with top resembling the old prairie schooners) is pulled across the stage, Left to Right, by one or two "mules" (actors in mule costumes, or in coveralls with faces made up like mules, with long ears). Inside the wagon is PECOS BILL, dressed in baby dress and bonnet (the same actor may play Bill throughout)]

ANNOUNCER. The family was very large–with so many children that the Mother and Daddy could hardly count them. When the wagon bounced over a rock, one of the children bounced out. *[BILL falls out the back of the wagon and lies on the stage floor]* Since the family had so many children, they never did miss the baby, and the wagon rolled on out of sight. *[It does. BILL lies on the floor and squawls like a baby]* Soon a Coyote came trotting down the path. *[COYOTE enters, Left, merrily jumping and hopping across the stage. COYOTE pantomimes what the Announcer says, performing the action* after *the Announcer reads it]* She heard the baby crying, but she didn't know where the sound was coming from. At first the Coyote was scared and hid behind a cactus. She peeped out and saw the baby, and jumped back to hide behind the cactus again. The baby squawled louder and louder. The Coyote peeped out again and decided to investigate. *[COYOTE tiptoes in big, exaggerated four-legged tiptoe steps to the baby]* The Coyote had never seen a human baby before and didn't know what it was.

COYOTE. *[Peering at baby]* What kind of animal are you? You don't look like a coyote. *[She leans over and smells the baby–then rises, holding her nose–the baby must need a diaper change]* Phooo-eeee–you don't smell like one either. Are you a bear? *[She pokes the baby with her front paw; the BABY lets out a terrific squawl and kicks aimlessly. One kick happens to catch the Coyote on the shin. COYOTE yelps and jumps around in pain, holding her leg]* Owwwwwwwwww!

ANNOUNCER. The Coyote just couldn't figure out what kind of animal this was–but she decided that it was crying because it was hungry.

What could she give the little fellow to eat? *[COYOTE looks around for food, spies a bone, holds it up]* She found a bone. A bone is a delicious delicacy for coyotes, so she figured this little creature would like to gnaw on the bone. *[COYOTE holds the bone to the baby, but it doesn't take it]*

COYOTE. What's the matter with you? This is a good bone. Looks like a skunk's bone. Try it. *[Tries to force the bone in the baby's mouth. No luck. COYOTE decides to eat the bone herself (it's really a cookie)]* Mmmm–good. Want some? *[Holds the bone out to the baby again–no luck. COYOTE finishes eating it. BABY howls louder than ever]*

ANNOUNCER. Not knowing what else to do, the Coyote decided to take the funny-looking creature home to mother. She'll know what to do. *[COYOTE grabs Bill's legs and pulls him offstage Right]* And sure enough, the Mama Coyote did know what to do. She gave the baby milk, and he grew and grew, and soon he could run and talk and play.

[BILL and COYOTE (and other Coyotes if desired) leap-frog over one another onto the stage. BILL is on all fours just like the coyotes. They chase each other, play tag, hide from one another, etc.]

COYOTE. This is fun, isn't it!

BILL. Yep. We coyotes really enjoy life!

ANNOUNCER. Yes, he thought he was a coyote. And why not? There were no mirrors to see himself in. And since the other coyotes walked on four feet, he did, too. It never occurred to him to try to stand on two feet. *[BILL and COYOTE continue playing and chase each other off Stage Left]* Living with animals and learning to fend for himself in the wilderness made the young man very strong. *[BILL enters, flexing his muscles like Mr. America]* He could outrun jackrabbits and he could wrestle with wolves and bears. And he could howl louder than any other coyote around. Every night when the moon came up, he would climb up on a big boulder and howl. *[BILL looks around for a big boulder, doesn't see one, runs offstage and returns carrying a huge, huge rock (made of foam rubber, styrofoam, papier-mache, or some other very light substance) in both hands. He places the rock at Down Center, climbs up on it, lifts his head like a coyote and lets out a howl that will have the audience holding its ears]* One day as the young man was wandering through the cactus looking for food, he spied a strange creature approaching him. *[SUE appears Left. BILL hides behind a cactus. He will act now much like the Coyote did when she found the baby]*

He finally found the courage to come out and confront this funny-looking animal. *[BILL and SUE meet at Center. BILL looks at her and then laughs vigorously]*

SUE. What's so funny?

BILL. You are. I've never seen such a funny-looking creature before. What kind of animal are you?

SUE. I'm a human. Just like you.

BILL. Human? What kind of animal is a human.

SUE. Well, for one thing, humans walk on two legs. Why are you crawling?

BILL. Crawling?

SUE. Sure. Stand up. That's what feet are for. *[She helps him to stand]*

BILL. *[He likes it. He dances a little jig. Then trots in place, like an athlete warming up. Then he waggles his hands, looking at them]* If we stand on those feet *[pointing to his feet]*, what are these feet for *[indicating his hands]*?

SUE. Those aren't feet, silly. They're hands.

BILL. What do you use hands for?

SUE. Why–to hold things, and–

BILL. I don't need hands to hold things. We coyotes hold everything in our mouths. *[He grabs the strap of her purse in his mouth and prances around on all fours]*

SUE. You're not a coyote, dummy–you're a person.

BILL. I thought you said I was a human.

SUE. You are–a human person. A man.

BILL. Well, I wish you'd make up your mind–am I a human or a person or a man?

SUE. You're all three. What's your name, anyway?

BILL. Pecos Coyote.

SUE. That's no name for a human. I'm going to call you Bill. My name's Sue.

BILL. Sue! Ha! Ha! Ha! That's a funny name.

SUE. *[She has never known anyone so dumb]* You'd better come home with me. You've got a lot to learn. I'll bet you've never even been to school. *[She takes his hand and begins leading him off Left]*

BILL. *[As they are disappearing]* School? What's that? I don't think I'll like it.

ANNOUNCER. Pecos Bill continued to grow stronger and stronger–

and smarter and smarter, too, because he did go to school—and he liked it. *[BILL enters, carrying a baseball bat and eating a candy bar]*

BILL. I like school—recess, and the cafeteria, and the snack bar—and— *[SUE runs across the stage]* chasing girls! *[He runs after her]*

ANNOUNCER. Bill returned to the place he grew up to visit his old friends now and then. *[BILL runs in Left, and COYOTE (and any other coyotes that appeared earlier) runs in Right. BILL gets on hands and knees. They hug and pat each other and play tag, etc. Their game carries them offstage]* One day while Pecos Bill was in the wilderness, a strange thing happened. *[We hear a horse's neigh. BILL comes on stage, listening and looking for the source of the sound]* Bill spotted a wild horse coming down the mountain. It was the biggest, fastest, meanest-looking horse he ever saw. *[HORSE (a tall, strong actor dressed in a horse's costume) runs in Right and gallops around the stage]* Bill decided to catch the horse and tame him. *[BILL runs after HORSE, hollering "whoa, whoa!" HORSE neighs. BILL's yells and HORSE's neighs get louder and wilder. BILL finally catches HORSE by the neck and hops on his back. HORSE bucks and snorts and neighs wildly, trying to throw Bill. BILL whoops and hollers and waves his cowboy hat in the air like a cowboy riding a bucking bronco at a rodeo]* Bill finally tamed the horse, and they became great friends. *[The HORSE begins walking calmly. BILL hugs Horse, and they exit Left]* Others tried to ride the horse, but no one except Bill could stay on him. And because many women lost husbands who tried to ride him, they named the horse Widowmaker. *[BILL enters leading the horse]*

BILL. You know, Widowmaker, I grew up on this sandy prairie. But it's so flat and ugly—why don't we make it into the most beautiful place in the world and name it Texas! *[WIDOWMAKER nods his head and paws the ground in ecstasy]* Hey, Widowmaker, look what you're doing! *[They look where WIDOWMAKER has been pawing. BILL reaches down (maybe behind a cactus) and scoops up water]* You just dug the Rio Grande!

ANNOUNCER. Widowmaker had kicked up so much sand, Bill had to take off his boots and empty them out. *[BILL takes off his boots and throws the "sand" upstage. A mountain appears (perhaps a stagehand can bring on a mountain profile and place it as a backdrop)]*

BILL. *[Pointing at mountain]* Look—the Davis Mountains! Well, let's dig some more rivers! *[WIDOWMAKER paws the ground, and BILL scoops up "dirt" with his hands. The action leads them offstage]*

ANNOUNCER. In one morning they dug the Pecos River and the Devil's River and the Llano, the San Antonio, and the Nueces. That afternoon Widowmaker pawed up the Comal, the Guadalupe, the Lavaca, and the Navidad, and swished out Woman Hollering Creek with his tail. Bill scooped out the Colorado, the Brazos, the Trinity, the San Jacinto, and the Sabine. Bill got thirsty and drew a bucket of water for a drink. He drank a couple of dipperfuls and threw the rest over his left shoulder —and the Red River was formed. All that digging was hard work, and Bill sweated a lot. *[BILL enters holding a drenched large bandanna]* He pulled out a bandanna about the size of Louisiana and wiped his face. Then he wrung out the bandanna *[he does]* and the Gulf of Mexico poured out. *[WIDOWMAKER comes trotting in. He has a frying pan and a couple of hotdogs strapped to his back]*

BILL. Well, Widowmaker, I guess it's about supper time.

WIDOWMAKER. Yup.

BILL. What do we have to eat? *[WIDOWMAKER motions to his back. BILL takes the frying pan, drops in the hotdogs, and mimes cooking over a fire]*

ANNOUNCER. They ate a couple of buffaloes for supper that night. They poured some lemon juice into Lake Texoma and washed the food down with lemonade. It took five wet Northers to fill the lake up again. Bill threw the frying pan over his right shoulder. It scooped out Palo Duro Canyon, and the handle pushed aside part of Oklahoma. So Texas has a Panhandle. And then Pecos Bill and Widowmaker lay down for a good night's sleep under the beautiful Texas sky.

BILL. Look at all those stars. I bet stars are prettier in the Texas sky than anywhere. *[WIDOWMAKER neighs in agreement]*

WIDOWMAKER. *[In a deep, horsey voice]* Wal, we've made us some rivers and a gulf and the Panhandle. What this State needs now is some cities.

BILL. You're right. Let's make some out of those stars.

ANNOUNCER. And so Pecos Bill reached up in the sky and plucked a big bright star. *[He can reach offstage and take a star from someone in the wings, or a star can descend from the loft and he can jump up and grab it. A stagehand pushes a large cut-out map of Texas onto the stage, and BILL puts the first star where San Antonio is located on the map. (Another way of handling this scene: BILL can mime grabbing stars and throwing them at the map. As each city is named, a gelatin-covered hole for that city may light up on the map)]* Bill whirled around and threw the star and it fell beside the Alamo, and the Fiesta City of San Antonio was born. *[A CHORUS dressed in Mexican peasant costumes may enter and sing a song about San Antonio (see Production Notes)]*

ANNOUNCER. When Pecos Bill reached for the second star, it slipped from his hands. One of the points hit Widowmaker in the flanks and the fiery bronco kicked it into stardust. A Texas tornado grabbed the stardust and settled it down in the shape of a Big D. And Bill named that city Dallas and thought of it ever afterward as a good place to have fun. *[CHORUS may enter in Dallas Cowboy football and cheerleader uniforms and sing a Dallas song]*

ANNOUNCER. The next star was intended to be a coastal city, but Pecos Bill dropped it 30 miles from the coast. Never daunted by trifles, Bill stuck his finger into the Southeast Texas mud and opened a ship channel to the Gulf. And Houston rose into the Texas sky. *[CHORUS in sailor costumes may sing]*

ANNOUNCER. Widowmaker wanted a gateway to the West, and so they found a star named Fort Worth. And they stuck in some gateways to Mexico, like Brownsville and Laredo, and El Paso. The Panhandle looked awfully lonely and bare, so they created Amarillo. And there were many other cities, like . . . *[Name some of your favorites, including your own city if it hasn't been named. CHORUS, dressed appropriately for your city, may sing]*

ANNOUNCER. Pecos Bill and Widowmaker looked at the map and thought a while.

WIDOWMAKER. This State needs a capital. Where we gonna put it?

BILL. How about deep in the heart of Texas!

ANNOUNCER. They found a big bright star and stuck it on the banks of the Colorado, and Austin came into being. *[CHORUS, in red, white, and blue costumes, may sing "Deep in the Heart of Texas," or any other appropriate song]*

ANNOUNCER. All this happened long, long ago, so Bill and Widowmaker aren't around any more. But they say that Pecos Bill never died, nor did he fade away. He figured that the best way to keep an eye on this State that he loved was to live up there among the stars. So he said to Widowmaker . . .

BILL. Think you can pitch me up there into the sky?

WIDOWMAKER. Sure–no problem at all. *[BILL hops on Widow-*

maker's back, and WIDOWMAKER starts pitching, bouncing Bill higher and higher as they exit Left]

ANNOUNCER. And so Widowmaker pitched and pitched . . . and if you look up on any clear night, you'll see Pecos Bill in the sky winking at you—and Texas. *[CHORUS in cowboy and cowgirl costumes may sing "The Eyes of Texas" or "Texas Our Texas" or any other appropriate song. If lights are used on the map, they can blink]*

CURTAIN

PRODUCTION NOTES

Properties

Texas Between the Rivers

Bow and arrow (may be toy)—Indian brave
Rolling pin—Indian squaw
Bandanna handkerchief—Frenchman
Treasure map—Spaniard
Survey map—Austin
Rifles—Dewees and Jim

Texas by Any Other Name

5 profile cut-outs of Texas (we suggest cutting them out of a 4′ x 4′ sheet of masonite, quarter-inch plywood, or other lightweight but stiff material). Each is lettered with one of the following names in letters large enough to be easily read by all members of the audience: See Fig. 3 under "The Set"

TEJAS
LOUISIANA
New Philippines
New Estremadura
COAHUILA AND

The letter X (to be placed over J of "Tejas")—Mexican peasant
Flags(optional)—French, Spanish, Mexican
Cane fishing pole—Fishing Pole Girl
Knife, napkin, and knife sharpening stick—Karankawa

A Capital Idea

Surveyor's chain—Helpers
Wooden hammer and peg—Bastrop
Survey map—Austin

It Takes a Heap of Lovin'

Old-fashioned carpenters tools (saws, hammers, planes)—Men
Sections of log cabin—on sawhorses (see "Set" below)
Ladles, bowls, spoons—Women
Bandanna handkerchiefs—Men

Life in the Country

Rifles—one for each Man
3 bowls of soup—Wives

Those Revolting Texians

Small cannon (may be chipboard or plywood cutout)—Soldiers
"Come and Take It" flag—Soldier (see Fig. 5 & 6)
Tree stumps (see "Set" below)
Knapsacks—Runaways
Biscuit—Runaway 1
Map—Houston

Three-Legged Willie

Stick of wood (for gavel)—Judge
Bowie knife—Man 1
Six-shooter—Judge

Pecos Bill and the Texas Stars

Covered wagon—a small wagon (may be a child's red wagon) with a canvas top shaped like the prairie schooners
Cookie shaped like a bone—Coyote
Huge boulder (made of foam rubber, styrofoam, or other light substance)—Bill
Baseball bat—Bill
Candy bar—Bill
Mountain (profile cut out of cardboard; or a canvas backdrop)
Water-saturated bandanna—Bill
Frying pan, hot dogs—Widowmaker
Map of Texas and stars

Costumes and Make-Up

The **Texans** in this play are depicted in scenes in the wilderness; hence they would not be "dressed up." Homemade garments of homemade material like buckskin, cotton, and wool would be authentic. **Stephen F. Austin** may be more formally dressed than the others. **Baron de Bastrop,** a native of Prussia, may be formally dressed even though he is working. **Sam Houston** may wear some symbol of his status as commander of the Texian Army. Photos of Houston, Austin, and pioneer men, women, and children are abundant in Texas history books, encyclopedias, etc. **Three-Legged Willie**'s trousers looked something like Fig. 1. The **Indians, Frenchmen,** and **Spaniards** may wear fanciful symbolic costumes or authentic clothing—as you desire. **Pecos Bill** may be dressed as a typical Hollywood-style Texas cowboy —white ten gallon hat, fancy shirt, khaki or blue jean trousers, chaps resembling cowhide, and high-heeled cowboy boots. **Widowmaker** and the **coyotes** and **mules** in "Pecos Bill" and the **deer** in "Texas Between the Rivers" may wear animal costumes or something nondescript, like jumpsuits, with facial make-up, and animal "accessories"—ears, tail, a mane for Widowmaker, and antlers for the deer. Suggestions are included in the text for dressing the **chorus** members to symbolize the cities they represent.

Fig. 1: Three-Legged Willie's special trousers

Lights, Sound, and Special Effects

As always, well-designed lighting effects enhance a stage production. However, the plays in this book may be presented on the floor in a large room, on an open-air platform, or virtually anywhere, with whatever light is available.

The "stars" on the map in "Pecos Bill and the Texas Stars" may be handled in various ways. A small lightbulb on an electric cord with its own switch, or with a plug to be inserted in a socket will do. A floodlight may be mounted behind the map, with each hole covered by a piece of cardboard. A stagehand behind the map can uncover each hole on cue. Instead of lighting each star, Pecos Bill may hang a glittery star at each place on the map.

The booming voice in "Texas Between the Rivers" may be effected by having the Announcer speak into an echo box or a cheerleader's megaphone—or taping the speeches in a small shower stall with tiles walls.

The dog's howl, bird calls, and forest sounds may all be found on sound effects records available from theatre supply firms.

The firing of the cannon in "Those Revolting Texians" requires special care for the sake of safety. Perhaps the safest way is to conceal a camera flashbulb in or behind the barrel and flash it on cue. A bass drum or tympano offstage may provide the sound. Smoke machines are available from theatre supply firms. Flash boxes are very effective, both for the cannon fire and for the war effects later in "Those Revolting Texians." However, flash boxes can be very dangerous if not handled properly. Flashbulbs exploded backstage can make satisfactory war effects.

Music

The amount of music—ranging from much to none, recorded or live—must be decided by each producer. The text recommends music with jungle sounds, like that written by the Brazilian composer Villa-Lobos, for the opening scene, followed by Indian tom-toms or chants. A few bars of the French national anthem (the Marseillaise) each time a Frenchman enters; Flamenco music each time a Spaniard enters; and recognizable Mexican music (like The Mexican Hat Dance or La Cucaracha) each time a Mexican enters would add flavor to the scenes.

Any type of early American hoe-down or dance music, like the Virginia Reel, may accompany the movements of the characters in "It Takes a Heap of Lovin'." A fiddler on stage playing the music live would be effective.

The chorus, or choruses, suggested for "Pecos Bill and the Texas Stars" may sing and/or dance to music appropriate for each city as its star appears on the map. Some suggestions: San Antonio Rose, On the Alamo, Mexican Hat Dance for San Antonio; Big D, "Dallas" TV show theme, or a football fight song for Dallas; Sailing, Sailing or other sea music for Houston; a song appropriate for your city, such as a well-known local school song; Deep in the Heart of Texas, Eyes of Texas, Texas Our Texas, etc., for Austin and for the finale.

Other background music and song and dance numbers may be added to any of the plays.

The Set

The plays in this book are designed to be performed on a bare stage, with set pieces added as needed:

Texas Between the Rivers—profile trees cut out of plywood, masonite, heavy cardboard, etc. and tacked to stage jacks or braces so they will be free standing. Four or five such trees placed at random in the upstage areas will give the right idea.

Pine tree laid out on 4'x8' sheet of plywood ←

Liveoak tree laid out on two 4'x8' sheets of plywood →

Fig. 2—Trees

Texas by Any Other Name—bare stage. Cut-out maps of Texas and flags if desired may be brought on—see Fig. 3.

A Capital Idea—one large liveoak tree—or a cut-out tree trunk reaching out of sight above the stage—will suffice. If desired, a backdrop painted with liveoaks and other trees along a river bank may be used.

It Takes a Heap of Lovin'—two sides and two roof sections of a log cabin lay on two or more sawhorses at Downstage Right as this scene opens. A large kettle suspended from a tripod is the center of the outdoor "kitchen" at Down Left. A table on which the dishes are placed may also be there. Several trees (the same ones used in previous scenes) may stand upstage. The sections of log cabin (constructed like stage flats and painted as illustrated here—Fig. 4) are set up at Upstage Center. A string attached to the top of the two walls and running offstage can be pulled to make the cabin collapse. It is important that the walls fall into each other; if they fall outward, the audience will be able to see the unpainted rear sides.

Fig. 3—Map of Texas laid on 4′x4′ sheet of plywood

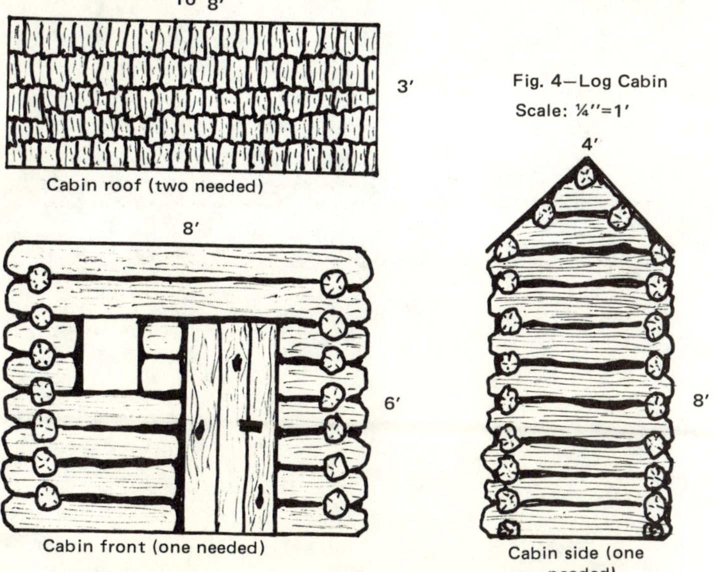

Cabin roof (two needed)

Cabin front (one needed)

Cabin side (one needed)

Fig. 4—Log Cabin
Scale: ¼″=1′

Life in the Country—the same log cabin used in the preceding scene may be used here—well braced this time. If it is impractical to have a door in the cabin, the inhabitants may enter from behind the cabin, as if the door was on the upstage side. Again, trees should be placed in the upper areas of the stage.

Those Revolting Texians—the "Come and Take It" cannon may be a plywood or cardboard cut-out; or a large PVC pipe or stovepipe may be used for the barrel, with the other parts cut out of plywood.

Fig. 5—Cannon

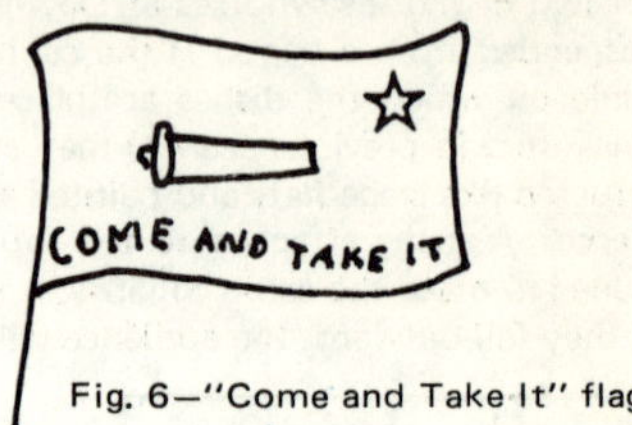

Fig. 6—"Come and Take It" flag

Tree stumps may be made by nailing cut-outs to small stools. More realistic stumps can be made by covering the sides of a stool with chicken wire shaped like a stump and then covering the chicken wire and seat of the stool with papier-mache. Trees or the riverbank backdrop mentioned above may be added to the Sam Houston scene.

Three-Legged Willie—a huge liveoak tree (or just the trunk reaching into the loft above the stage, as suggested above). Downstage of the tree are a wooden barrel and a stool. For added effect, a charred remains of a cabin wall and a charred tree trunk may be placed in the background.

Pecos Bill and the Texas Stars—several cut-out cactus plants, and the large map of Texas as suggested in the text.